D0067792

BEST OF
CHINA

Consultant Editor:
Valerie Ferguson

HERMES
HOUSE

Contents

Introduction   4

Flavourings & Spices   6

Techniques   8

Soups & Starters   10

Fish & Seafood   24

Poultry & Meat   38

Vegetarian & Side Dishes   52

Index   64

Introduction

The Chinese have perfected the art of rapid cooking over a period of many centuries. They invented the wok, which ensured ingredients cooked quickly and evenly. This, coincidentally, helped to preserve the colour, texture, flavour and nutrients of the food.

Stir-frying is the best-known Chinese cooking technique. The ingredients are chopped, sliced or shredded into even-size pieces and then fried in sizzling hot oil in which they are constantly tossed and stirred. The wok is also ideal for other fast-food techniques, such as deep frying and steaming. Bamboo steamers are available in a range of sizes from kitchenware shops and Chinese supermarkets.

In Chinese cooking, the emphasis is on quality and freshness: cuts of meat should be lean and tender and vegetables and herbs bright and fresh.

The recipes in this book include favourites, such as Hot & Sour Soup and Pork Chow Mein, and more unusual dishes, such as Three Sea Flavours Stir-fry. All can be cooked in less than 20 minutes. The ingredients are generally available from large supermarkets and Chinese food stores, so you can easily enjoy the authentic taste of Chinese cooking in your home.

Flavourings & Spices

You can now obtain Chinese ingredients from most supermarkets.

BLACK BEAN PRODUCTS
Black bean sauce or paste is made from salted fermented soy beans, mixed to a paste with flavourings. It is highly concentrated and usually added at the start of cooking to release the flavour. A sweet version is also available. Preserved black beans are very salty and pungent.

CHILLIES, FRESH & DRIED
A wide variety of these hot capsicums is available. Sweet chilli sauce is made from chillies, vinegar, sugar and salt. Use sparingly for cooking and dipping. Chilli bean paste is made from fermented bean paste with hot chillies added.

CHINESE RICE WINE
Shaohsing wine is reputedly the finest variety. It has a rich, sherry-like flavour.

CHINESE SESAME PASTE
This has a stronger flavour than the Middle Eastern version.

FIVE-SPICE POWDER
A finely ground mixture of fennel seeds, star anise, Sichuan peppercorns, cloves and cinnamon. It has a fairly strong liquorice taste and a pungent aroma and should be used sparingly during cooking.

GARLIC
This aromatic vegetable is one of the most important flavourings in Chinese cooking. The most common way of preparing garlic is to peel it, then chop it finely or mince it in a garlic press.

Below, clockwise from top left: Yellow bean sauce, black bean sauce, oyster sauce, dark and light soy sauces and hoisin sauce.

Above: Garlic, fresh root ginger, red and green, dried and fresh chillies are essential Chinese ingredients.

GINGER

Fresh root ginger is an essential flavouring ingredient in Chinese cooking. It is peeled, then sliced, shredded or minced before use. It can also be pickled.

HOISIN SAUCE

A thick, rich, dark sauce often used for flavouring meat and poultry before cooking, or in a dipping sauce.

OYSTER SAUCE

This thick, dark sauce is made from oyster juice, flour, salt and sugar. It is usually added at the end of cooking.

PLUM SAUCE

This has a unique fruity flavour with a sweet and sour taste.

RICE VINEGAR

A colourless, slightly sweet vinegar used to add sharpness to sweet-and-sour dishes. If rice vinegar is not obtainable, use white wine vinegar or cider vinegar sweetened with sugar.

SESAME OIL

This aromatic oil is made from roasted sesame seeds. Small quantities are used at the end of cooking.

SICHUAN PEPPERCORNS

Red aromatic peppercorns which are best used roasted and ground.

SOY SAUCE (LIGHT & DARK)

This is made from fermented soy beans, yeast, salt and sugar. Light soy sauce is a thin sauce used for flavouring and also as a table accompaniment. The flavour is lighter and fresher than dark soy sauce, but a little more salty.

Techniques

GENERAL RULES FOR STIR-FRYING

Stir-frying takes very little cooking time, often only minutes. For this reason it is important that all the ingredients are prepared ahead of time and cut to the same shape and size.

1 Always preheat the wok for a few minutes. If adding oil, swirl it into the wok and allow it to heat up before adding the next ingredients.

2 When adding the first ingredients, reduce the heat a little to ensure they are not overcooked or burnt.

4 Use a long-handled scoop or spatula to keep the ingredients turning as you stir-fry them. This will allow the ingredients to cook as evenly and quickly as possible.

3 Once all the ingredients have been added, quickly increase the heat. This allows them to retain a crisp, fresh texture, and prevents sogginess.

5 It may be easier to slice any meat that is to be used for stir-frying if it has been frozen slightly for an hour or so beforehand. By the time you have sliced it, the meat will be sufficiently thawed for it to be cooked in the usual way.

SEASONING YOUR WOK

If you are using a new wok, which is not a non-stick variety, you will need to prepare it as follows, to ensure the best results.

1 Heat the wok with 30–45 ml/ 2–3 tbsp salt for about 15 minutes, stirring so that the whole surface is coated with the salt. Wipe out the salt and continue to use as recommended.

2 To clean your wok after using, allow the wok to cool slightly then wipe out the inside with kitchen paper. Where possible, keep washing with detergent to a minimum as this removes the non-stick surface.

3 If your wok is not non-stick you can also wipe a little groundnut oil around the inside before storing it away. A naturally seasoned pan will create a good non-stick surface.

BASIC STOCK

The basic stock is used not only as the basis for soup making, but also for general use in cooking.

Makes 2.25 litres/4 pints/ 10 cups

INGREDIENTS

675 g/1½ lb chicken pieces
675 g/1½ lb pork spare ribs
3.25 litres/6 pints/15 cups cold water
3–4 pieces of fresh root ginger, unpeeled and crushed
3–4 spring onions, each tied into a knot
45–60 ml/3–4 tbsp Chinese rice wine or dry sherry

1 Trim off any excess fat from the chicken and spare ribs and chop them into large pieces. Place the pieces in a large saucepan with the water. Add the ginger and spring onion.

2 Bring the water to the boil and skim off the froth that forms on the surface. Reduce the heat and simmer, uncovered, for 2–3 hours.

3 Strain the stock, discarding the meat, ginger and spring onions. Add the wine or sherry and return to the boil. Simmer for 2–3 minutes. Cool, then refrigerate. It will keep for up to 4–5 days. Alternatively, the stock can be frozen in small containers and thawed when required.

Corn & Crabmeat Soup

This is a popular soup in Chinese restaurants. You must use creamed corn in the recipe to achieve the right consistency.

Serves 4

INGREDIENTS
115 g/4 oz crabmeat
2.5 ml/½ tsp finely chopped fresh
    root ginger
2 egg whites
30 ml/2 tbsp milk
15 ml/1 tbsp cornflour paste
600 ml/1 pint/2½ cups
    Basic Stock
225 g/8 oz can creamed corn
salt and freshly ground black pepper
finely chopped spring onions,
    to garnish

1 In a bowl, flake the crabmeat with chopsticks or a fork. Add the chopped fresh root ginger, and stir well to combine.

COOK'S TIP: To make cornflour paste, combine 4 parts cornflour with 5 parts water.

2 Beat the egg whites for a few seconds until frothy, add the milk and cornflour paste and beat again until smooth. Blend with the flaked crabmeat.

3 Bring the stock to the boil in a wok, add the creamed sweetcorn and bring back to the boil once more.

4 Stir in the crabmeat and egg-white mixture, adjust the seasoning and stir gently until well blended. Serve the soup garnished with finely chopped spring onions.

Hot & Sour Soup

This must be the all-time favourite Chinese soup throughout the world. It is easy to make once you have got all the necessary ingredients together.

Serves 4

INGREDIENTS
4–6 dried Chinese mushrooms, soaked
115 g/4 oz pork or chicken
1 cake tofu (beancurd)
50 g/2 oz sliced bamboo shoots, drained
600 ml/1 pint/2½ cups Basic Stock
15 ml/1 tbsp Chinese rice wine or dry sherry
15 ml/1 tbsp light soy sauce
15 ml/1 tbsp rice vinegar
2.5 ml/½ tsp freshly ground white pepper
15 ml/1 tbsp cornflour paste
salt

1 Squeeze the soaked mushrooms dry, then discard the hard stalks. Thinly shred the mushrooms, meat, tofu and bamboo shoots.

2 Bring the stock to a rolling boil in a wok and add the shredded ingredients. Bring back to the boil and simmer for about 1 minute.

3 Add the seasonings to taste and bring back to the boil once more. Add the cornflour paste and stir until thickened. Serve hot.

Egg Flower Soup

When the egg is stirred in, it sets into pretty strands giving the soup a flowery look, hence the name.

Serves 6

INGREDIENTS

1 litre/1¾ pints/4 cups Basic Stock
45 ml/3 tbsp light soy sauce
30 ml/2 tbsp Chinese rice wine or
    dry sherry
3 spring onions, diagonally sliced
small piece of fresh root ginger, shredded
4 large lettuce leaves, shredded
5 ml/1 tsp sesame oil
2 eggs, beaten
salt and freshly ground black pepper
sesame seeds, to garnish

1 Pour the stock into a saucepan. Add all the ingredients except the eggs, seeds and seasoning. Bring to the boil and cook for about 2 minutes.

2 Very carefully, pour the eggs in a thin, steady stream into the centre of the boiling liquid.

3 Count to three, then quickly stir the soup. The egg will begin to cook and form long threads. Season to taste, ladle into warm bowls and serve, sprinkled with sesame seeds.

Seafood Wontons with Coriander Dressing

Wontons are small dumplings that may be poached, as here, fried or steamed. Water chestnuts add a light crunch to the filling.

Serves 4

INGREDIENTS
225 g/8 oz raw prawns, peeled
    and deveined
115 g/4 oz white crabmeat,
    picked over
4 canned water chestnuts,
    finely diced
1 spring onion, finely chopped
1 small green chilli, seeded and
    finely chopped
2.5 ml/½ tsp grated fresh
    root ginger
1 egg, separated
20–24 wonton wrappers
salt and freshly ground black pepper
coriander leaves, to garnish

FOR THE CORIANDER DRESSING
30 ml/2 tbsp rice vinegar
15 ml/1 tbsp chopped pickled ginger
90 ml/6 tbsp olive oil
15 ml/1 tbsp soy sauce
45 ml/3 tbsp chopped fresh coriander
30 ml/2 tbsp finely diced
    red pepper

2 Place a wonton wrapper on a board. Put about 5 ml/1 tsp of the filling just above the centre. Brush the edges of the wrapper with a little egg yolk. Bring the bottom of the wrapper up over the filling. Press gently to expel any air, then seal in a triangle.

1 Finely dice the prawns and place them in a bowl. Add the crabmeat, water chestnuts, spring onion, chilli, ginger and egg white. Season and stir the mixture well.

3 Bring the two side points up over the filling, overlap them and pinch the ends firmly together. Space the filled wontons on a large baking sheet lined with greaseproof paper.

4 Bring a large saucepan half-filled with water to simmering point. Add the filled wontons, a few at a time, and simmer for 2–3 minutes. When ready, the wrappers will be translucent and the filling cooked. Remove with a slotted spoon, drain briefly, then spread on trays. Keep warm while cooking the rest.

5 Make the coriander dressing by placing all the ingredients together in a bowl and whisking until thoroughly combined.

6 Divide the wontons among serving dishes, drizzle with the coriander dressing and serve immediately, garnished with a handful of coriander leaves.

Crispy "Seaweed" with Flaked Almonds

This popular starter in Chinese restaurants is, in fact, usually made not with seaweed, but spring greens!

Serves 4–6

INGREDIENTS
450 g/1 lb spring greens
groundnut oil, for deep frying
1.5 ml/¼ tsp sea salt flakes
5 ml/1 tsp caster sugar
50 g/2 oz/½ cup flaked
   almonds, toasted

1 Wash the spring greens under plenty of cold, running water and then pat dry with kitchen paper. Remove and discard the thick white stalks from the spring greens, leaving just the leaves.

3 Half-fill a wok with oil and heat to 180°C/350°F. Deep fry the spring greens, in batches, for about 1 minute, until they darken and crisp. Remove each batch from the wok as soon as it is ready and drain on kitchen paper.

2 Lay several of the spring green leaves on top of one another, roll them up tightly and, using a sharp knife, slice the leaves as finely as possible into thread-like strips.

4 Transfer the "seaweed" to a serving dish, sprinkle with the salt and sugar, then mix well. Garnish with the toasted flaked almonds scattered over.

Crab Spring Rolls & Hoisin Dipping Sauce

If you are unable to find spring roll wrappers, use filo pastry. In both cases, keep the wrappers – and the filled rolls – covered with clear film.

Serves 4–6

INGREDIENTS
15 ml/1 tbsp groundnut oil
5 ml/1 tsp sesame oil
1 garlic clove, crushed
1 fresh red chilli, seeded and
    finely sliced
450 g/1 lb pack fresh stir-fry vegetables
2.5 cm/1 in piece of fresh
    root ginger, grated
15 ml/1 tbsp Chinese rice wine or
    dry sherry
15 ml/1 tbsp soy sauce
350 g/12 oz fresh dressed crabmeat (brown
    and white meat)
12 spring roll wrappers
1 small egg, beaten
oil, for deep frying
salt and freshly ground black pepper
lime wedges and fresh coriander,
    to garnish

FOR THE DIPPING SAUCE
4 spring onions
2 red chillies, seeded
60 ml/4 tbsp hoisin sauce
120 ml/4 fl oz/½ cup passata
4 cm/1½ in piece of fresh root ginger,
    finely chopped
2 garlic cloves, finely chopped
5 ml/1 tsp sesame oil (optional)
spring onion and red chilli slices, to garnish

1 First make the dipping sauce. Trim off and discard the green parts of the spring onions and thinly slice the remainder. Finely slice the chillies widthways into tiny strips. Stir together the hoisin sauce, passata, spring onions, ginger, chillies, garlic and sesame oil, if using. Set aside until required, but for no longer than 1 hour.

2 Preheat a wok, then add the groundnut and sesame oils. When hot, stir-fry the crushed garlic and chilli for 1 minute. Add the vegetables and ginger and stir-fry for 1 minute more, then drizzle over the rice wine or sherry and soy sauce. Allow the mixture to bubble up for 1 minute.

3 Using a slotted spoon, transfer the vegetables to a dish. Set aside until cool, then stir in the crabmeat and season with salt and pepper.

4 Soften the spring roll wrappers, following the directions on the packet. Place some of the filling on a wrapper, fold over the front edge and the sides and roll up neatly, sealing the edges with a little beaten egg. Repeat this process with the remaining wrappers and filling.

5 Heat the oil in the wok and fry the rolls in batches, turning, until brown and crisp. Remove with a slotted spoon, drain on kitchen paper and keep hot while frying the remainder. Serve at once, garnished with lime wedges and coriander, with the garnished hoisin dipping sauce.

Red Snapper with Ginger & Spring Onions

This is a classic Chinese way of cooking fish. Pouring the hot oil over the spring onions and ginger partly cooks them, enhancing their flavour.

Serves 2–3

INGREDIENTS

1 red snapper, about 675–900 g/1½–2 lb, cleaned and scaled with head left on
1 bunch spring onions, cut into thin shreds
2.5 cm/1 in piece of fresh root ginger, cut into thin shreds
1.5 ml/¼ tsp salt
1.5 ml/¼ tsp caster sugar
45 ml/3 tbsp groundnut oil
5 ml/1 tsp sesame oil
30–45 ml/2–3 tbsp light soy sauce
spring onion brushes, to garnish

1 Rinse the fish, then pat dry. Slash diagonally, three times on each side. Set on a heatproof oval plate that will fit inside a steamer.

2 Tuck one-third of the spring onions and ginger inside the fish. Place the plate inside the steamer, cover and place in a wok.

3 Place over a medium heat to steam for 10–15 minutes, until the fish flakes easily when it is tested with the tip of a knife.

4 Remove the plate from the steamer. Sprinkle over the salt, sugar and remaining spring onions and ginger.

5 Heat the groundnut and sesame oils in a small pan until very hot, then slowly pour over the fish.

6 Drizzle over the soy sauce and serve at once, garnished with spring onion brushes.

COOK'S TIP: If the fish is too big to fit inside the steamer, cut off the head and place it alongside the body – it can then be reassembled, after it is cooked, for serving.

Fish with Sweet & Sour Sauce

Another, rather charming, name for this dish is Five-willow Fish, after the five shredded ingredients in the dressing.

Serves 4–6

INGREDIENTS
1 carp, bream, sea bass, trout, grouper
   or grey mullet, weighing about
   675 g/1½ lb, gutted
5 ml/1 tsp salt
about 30 ml/2 tbsp plain flour
vegetable oil, for deep frying
fresh coriander leaves, to garnish

FOR THE SAUCE
15 ml/1 tbsp vegetable oil
50 g/2 oz carrot, thinly shredded
50 g/2 oz sliced bamboo shoots,
   drained and shredded
25 g/1 oz green pepper, thinly shredded
25 g/1 oz red pepper, thinly shredded
2–3 spring onions, thinly shredded
15 ml/1 tbsp thinly shredded fresh
   root ginger
15 ml/1 tbsp light soy sauce
30 ml/2 tbsp light brown sugar
30–45 ml/2–3 tbsp rice vinegar
about 120 ml/4 fl oz/½ cup Basic Stock
15 ml/1 tbsp cornflour paste

1 Clean and dry the fish well. Using a sharp knife, score both sides of the fish down to the bone with diagonal cuts at intervals of about 2.5 cm/1 in.

2 Rub the whole fish with salt both inside and out, then coat it from head to tail with flour.

3 Heat the oil for deep frying to 180°C/350°F. Deep fry the fish for about 3–4 minutes on both sides, or until it is golden brown all over. Remove the fish and drain well, then place on a heated platter.

4 For the sauce, heat the oil and stir-fry all the vegetables for about 1 minute, then add the seasoning. Blend well, add the stock and bring to the boil. Add the cornflour paste, stirring well until the sauce thickens and is smooth. Pour the sauce over the fish and garnish with coriander leaves.

Braised Whole Fish in Chilli & Garlic Sauce

This is a classic Sichuan recipe. In restaurants, the fish's head and tail are usually discarded before cooking, to be used in other dishes.

Serves 4–6

INGREDIENTS
1 carp, bream, sea bass, trout, grouper
    or grey mullet, weighing about
    675 g/1½ lb, gutted
15 ml/1 tbsp light soy sauce
15 ml/1 tbsp Chinese rice wine or
    dry sherry
vegetable oil, for deep frying

FOR THE SAUCE
2 garlic cloves, finely chopped
2–3 spring onions, finely chopped with
    the white and green parts separated,
    plus extra slices, to garnish
5 ml/1 tsp finely chopped fresh
    root ginger
30 ml/2 tbsp chilli bean sauce
15 ml/1 tbsp tomato purée
10 ml/2 tsp light brown sugar
15 ml/1 tbsp rice vinegar
about 120 ml/4 fl oz/½ cup Basic Stock
15 ml/1 tbsp cornflour paste
few drops sesame oil

1 Rinse and dry the fish well. Using a sharp knife, score both sides of the fish as far down as the bone with diagonal cuts about 2.5 cm/1 in apart. Rub the whole fish with soy sauce and wine or sherry on both sides, then leave to marinate for 10 minutes.

2 Heat the oil for deep frying in a wok. Deep fry the fish for about 3–4 minutes on both sides, or until golden brown.

3 Pour off the excess oil, leaving about 15 ml/1 tbsp in the wok. Push the fish to one side of the wok and add the garlic, the white part of the spring onions, ginger, chilli bean sauce, tomato purée, light brown sugar, rice vinegar and stock.

4 Bring to the boil and braise the fish in the sauce for 4–5 minutes, turning it over once.

5 Add the remaining spring onions to the pan and thicken the sauce with the cornflour paste. Remove from the pan and serve, sprinkled with the sesame oil and extra spring onion.

Three Sea Flavours Stir-fry

The delectable seafood combination in this dish is enhanced by the use of fresh root ginger and spring onions.

Serves 4

INGREDIENTS
4 large scallops, with the corals
225 g/8 oz firm white fish fillet, such as
    monkfish or cod
115 g/4 oz raw tiger prawns
300 ml/½ pint/1¼ cups fish stock
15 ml/1 tbsp vegetable oil
2 garlic cloves, coarsely chopped
5 cm/2 in piece of fresh root ginger,
    thinly sliced
8 spring onions, cut into 4 cm/1½ in pieces
30 ml/2 tbsp Chinese rice wine or
    dry sherry
5 ml/1 tsp cornflour
15 ml/1 tbsp cold water
salt and freshly ground white pepper
noodles or rice, to serve

2 Bring the fish stock to the boil in a pan. Add the seafood, lower the heat and poach the seafood gently for 1–2 minutes, until the fish, scallops and corals are just firm and the prawns have turned pink. Drain the seafood, reserving about 60 ml/4 tbsp of the stock for the sauce.

1 Separate the corals and slice each scallop in half horizontally. Cut the fish fillet into bite-size chunks. Peel and devein the prawns.

3 Heat the oil in a frying pan or wok over a high heat until very hot. Stir-fry the garlic, ginger and spring onions for a few seconds.

4 Add the seafood and rice wine or sherry. Stir-fry for 1 minute, then add the reserved stock and allow to simmer for 2 minutes.

5 Mix the cornflour to a paste with the water. Add the mixture to the pan or wok and cook, stirring gently, until the sauce thickens.

6 Season the stir-fry with salt and freshly ground white pepper to taste. Serve at once, with noodles or rice.

COOK'S TIP: It is important not to allow the seafood to overcook when poaching in the stock, or it will become tough and rubbery.

27

Stir-fried Prawns with Mangetouts

Prawns and mangetouts make a pretty dish, served with noodles.

Serves 4

INGREDIENTS
300 ml/½ pint/1¼ cups
   fish stock
350 g/12 oz raw tiger prawns, peeled
   and deveined
15 ml/1 tbsp vegetable oil
1 garlic clove, finely chopped
225 g/8 oz/2 cups mangetouts
1.5 ml/¼ tsp salt
15 ml/1 tbsp Chinese rice wine or
   dry sherry
15 ml/1 tbsp oyster sauce
5 ml/1 tsp cornflour
5 ml/1 tsp caster sugar
15 ml/1 tbsp cold water
1.5 ml/¼ tsp sesame oil

2 Heat the oil in a frying pan or wok. Fry the garlic for a few seconds, then add the mangetouts. Sprinkle with salt. Stir-fry for 1 minute.

1 Bring the fish stock to the boil in a frying pan. Add the prepared prawns. Allow to cook gently for 2 minutes, until the prawns have turned pink, then drain and set aside.

3 Add the prawns and rice wine or sherry to the pan or wok. Stir-fry briefly, then add the oyster sauce.

4 Mix the cornflour and sugar to a paste with the water. Add to the pan and cook, stirring constantly, until the sauce thickens slightly. Drizzle with sesame oil and serve.

Stir-fried Five-spice Squid with Black Bean Sauce

Squid is perfect for stir-frying as it should be cooked quickly. The spicy sauce makes the ideal accompaniment.

Serves 6

INGREDIENTS
450 g/1 lb small cleaned squid
45 ml/3 tbsp oil
2.5 cm/1 in piece of fresh root ginger, grated
1 garlic clove, crushed
8 spring onions, cut diagonally into 2.5 cm/
　1 in lengths
1 red pepper, seeded and cut into strips
1 fresh green chilli, seeded and thinly sliced
6 mushrooms, sliced
5 ml/1 tsp five-spice powder
30 ml/2 tbsp black bean sauce
30 ml/2 tbsp soy sauce
5 ml/1 tsp sugar
15 ml/1 tbsp Chinese rice wine or dry sherry

2 Preheat a wok briefly and add the oil. When hot, stir-fry the squid quickly. Remove with a slotted spoon and set aside. Add the ginger, garlic, spring onions, red pepper, chilli and mushrooms to the oil left in the wok and stir-fry for 2 minutes.

1 Rinse the squid and pull away the outer skin. Dry on kitchen paper. Using a sharp knife slit the squid open and score the outside into diamonds. Cut the squid into strips.

3 Return the squid to the wok and stir in the five-spice powder. Stir in the remaining ingredients. Bring to the boil and cook, stirring, for 1 minute. Serve immediately.

"Kung Po" Chicken – Sichuan Style

Kung Po was the name of a court official in Sichuan; his cook created this deliciously spicy dish of chicken and cashew nuts.

Serves 4

INGREDIENTS
350 g/12 oz chicken thigh, boned
   and skinned
1.5 ml/¼ tsp salt
½ egg white, lightly beaten
10 ml/2 tsp cornflour paste
1 medium green pepper
60 ml/4 tbsp vegetable oil
3–4 whole dried red chillies, soaked
   in water for 10 minutes
1 spring onion, cut into short sections
few small pieces of fresh
   root ginger, peeled
15 ml/1 tbsp sweet bean paste or
   hoisin sauce
5 ml/1 tsp chilli bean paste
15 ml/1 tbsp Chinese rice wine or
  dry sherry
115 g/4 oz/1½ cups roasted cashew nuts
few drops sesame oil

3 Heat the oil in a preheated wok. Stir-fry the chicken cubes for about 1 minute, or until the colour changes. Remove with a slotted spoon and keep warm.

1 Cut the prepared chicken meat into small cubes, each about the size of a sugar lump. In a bowl mix the chicken with the salt, beaten egg white and the cornflour paste.

2 Core and seed the green pepper and cut the flesh into cubes that are about the same size as the pieces of chicken.

4 Add the green pepper, dried red chillies, spring onion and ginger and stir-fry for about 1 minute. Add the chicken with the bean pastes or sauce and rice wine or sherry. Blend and cook for 1 minute, then add the nuts and sesame oil. Serve hot.

Shredded Chicken with Celery

A delightful contrast of textures.

Serves 4

INGREDIENTS
275 g/10 oz chicken breast fillet, skinned
5 ml/1 tsp salt
½ egg white, lightly beaten
10 ml/2 tsp cornflour paste
about 475 ml/16 fl oz/2 cups vegetable oil
1 celery heart, thinly shredded
1–2 fresh red chillies, seeded
   and shredded
1 spring onion, thinly shredded
few strips of fresh root ginger, thinly shredded
5 ml/1 tsp light brown sugar
15 ml/1 tbsp Chinese rice wine or
   dry sherry
few drops of sesame oil

1 Thinly shred the chicken. Mix with a pinch of the salt, the egg white and the cornflour paste.

2 Heat the oil in a preheated wok, add the chicken and stir to separate. When white, remove and drain. Keep warm. Pour off all but 30 ml/2 tbsp of the oil. Stir-fry the celery, chillies, spring onion and ginger for 1 minute. Add the chicken, salt, sugar and rice wine or sherry. Cook for 1 minute, add the sesame oil and serve.

Chicken with Chinese Vegetables

Also try pork, beef or prawns.

Serves 4

INGREDIENTS
225–275 g/8–10 oz boneless, skinless chicken
5 ml/1 tsp salt
½ egg white, lightly beaten
10 ml/2 tsp cornflour paste
60 ml/4 tbsp vegetable oil
6–8 small dried Chinese mushrooms, soaked
115 g/4 oz sliced bamboo shoots, drained
115 g/4 oz mangetouts, trimmed
1 spring onion, cut into short sections
few small pieces of fresh root ginger, peeled
5 ml/1 tsp light brown sugar
15 ml/1 tbsp light soy sauce
15 ml/1 tbsp Chinese rice wine or dry sherry
few drops of sesame oil

1 Cut the chicken into thin slices. Mix with a pinch of the salt, the egg white and the cornflour paste.

2 Heat the oil in a preheated wok, stir-fry the chicken for 30 seconds, remove and keep warm. Stir-fry the vegetables for 1 minute. Add the salt, sugar and chicken. Blend, then add the soy sauce and rice wine or sherry. Stir, sprinkle with sesame oil and serve.

Right: Shredded Chicken with Celery (top), Chicken with Chinese Vegetables

Stir-fried Crispy Duck

This stir-fry would be delicious wrapped in steamed Chinese pancakes, with a little extra warm plum sauce.

Serves 2

INGREDIENTS

275–350 g/10–12 oz boneless duck breast
30 ml/2 tbsp plain flour
60 ml/4 tbsp oil
1 bunch spring onions, halved lengthways
    and cut into 5 cm/2 in strips
275 g/10 oz/2½ cups finely shredded
    green cabbage
225 g/8 oz can water chestnuts, drained
    and sliced
50 g/2 oz/⅓ cup unsalted
    cashew nuts
115 g/4 oz cucumber, cut into strips
45 ml/3 tbsp plum sauce
15 ml/1 tbsp light soy sauce
salt and freshly ground black pepper
sliced spring onions, to garnish

2 Heat the oil in a preheated wok or large frying pan and cook the duck over a high heat until golden and crisp. Keep stirring to prevent the duck from sticking. Remove the duck pieces with a slotted spoon and drain them on kitchen paper. You may need to do this in batches.

3 Add the strips of spring onion to the wok or frying pan and cook for 2 minutes. Stir in the shredded cabbage and cook for 5 minutes, or until softened and golden.

4 Return the duck to the pan with the water chestnuts, cashews and cucumber. Stir-fry for 2 minutes.

1 Trim a little of the fat from the duck and thinly slice the meat. Season the flour well and use it to coat each piece of duck.

5 Add the plum sauce and soy sauce to the wok or pan with plenty of seasoning and heat for 2 minutes. Serve the duck piping hot, garnished with sliced spring onions.

Sweet & Sour Pork

This is a great idea for a quick family supper. Remember to cut the carrots into thin strips so that they cook in time.

Serves 4

INGREDIENTS
450 g/1 lb pork fillet
30 ml/2 tbsp plain flour
45 ml/3 tbsp oil
1 onion, roughly chopped
1 garlic clove, crushed
1 green pepper, cored, seeded
   and sliced
350 g/12 oz carrots, cut into strips
225 g/8 oz can bamboo
   shoots, drained
15 ml/1 tbsp white wine vinegar
15 ml/1 tbsp soft brown sugar
10 ml/2 tsp tomato purée
30 ml/2 tbsp light soy sauce
120 ml/4 fl oz/½ cup water
salt and freshly ground
   black pepper

2 Heat the oil in a preheated wok or large frying pan and cook the pork slices over a medium heat for about 5 minutes, until they are golden and cooked through. Remove the pork with a slotted spoon and drain on kitchen paper. You may need to do this in several batches.

1 Using a sharp knife, thinly slice the pork. Season the flour with salt and pepper and toss the pork in it to coat each piece thoroughly.

3 Add the onion and garlic to the wok or frying pan and cook for 3 minutes. Stir in the pepper and carrots and stir-fry over a high heat for 6–8 minutes, or until the vegetables are beginning to soften slightly.

4 Return the meat to the wok or pan with the bamboo shoots. Add the white wine vinegar, sugar, tomato purée, light soy sauce and water and bring to the boil. Allow the mixture to simmer gently for 2–3 minutes, or until it is piping hot. Adjust the seasoning, if necessary, and serve immediately.

Ginger Pork with Black Bean Sauce

The spicy ginger counterbalances the rich pork in this classic dish.

Serves 4

INGREDIENTS
350 g/12 oz pork fillet
1 garlic clove, crushed
15 ml/1 tbsp grated fresh root ginger
90 ml/6 tbsp chicken stock
30 ml/2 tbsp Chinese rice wine or dry sherry
15 ml/1 tbsp light soy sauce
5 ml/1 tsp sugar
10 ml/2 tsp cornflour
45 ml/3 tbsp groundnut oil
4 peppers (2 yellow, 2 red), cored, seeded
    and cut into strips
1 bunch spring onions, diagonally sliced
45 ml/3 tbsp preserved black beans,
    coarsely chopped
coriander sprigs, to garnish

1 Cut the pork into thin slices across the grain. Place in a dish and mix with the garlic and ginger. Marinate at room temperature for 15 minutes.

2 Blend together the stock, rice wine or sherry, soy sauce, sugar and cornflour in a small bowl and set aside.

3 Heat the oil in a preheated wok or large frying pan, add the pork and stir-fry for 2–3 minutes. Add the peppers and spring onions and stir-fry for a further 2 minutes.

4 Add the beans and sauce mixture and cook, stirring until thick. Serve hot, garnished with coriander.

Pork & Pepper Chow Mein

This speedy meal is flavoured with sesame oil for an authentic Chinese taste.

Serves 4

INGREDIENTS
175 g/6 oz medium egg noodles
350 g/12 oz pork fillet
30 ml/2 tbsp sunflower oil
15 ml/1 tbsp sesame oil
2 garlic cloves, crushed
8 spring onions, sliced
1 red pepper, cored, seeded and
  roughly chopped
1 green pepper, cored, seeded and
  roughly chopped
30 ml/2 tbsp dark soy sauce
45 ml/3 tbsp Chinese rice wine or dry sherry
175 g/6 oz/¾ cup beansprouts
45 ml/3 tbsp chopped fresh flat leaf parsley
15 ml/1 tbsp toasted sesame seeds

1 Soak the noodles in boiling water according to the packet instructions. Drain well. Thinly slice the pork fillet. Heat the sunflower oil in a preheated wok or large frying pan and cook the pork over a high heat, stirring, until golden brown and cooked through.

2 Add the sesame oil with the garlic, spring onions and peppers. Cook over a high heat for 3–4 minutes. Lower the heat and stir in the noodles, soy sauce and rice wine or sherry. Stir-fry for 2 minutes. Add the beansprouts and cook for 1–2 minutes. Stir in the parsley and serve sprinkled with the sesame seeds.

Stir-fried Pork with Vegetables

This is a basic recipe that is easily adapted for cooking any meat with any vegetables, according to seasonal availability.

Serves 4

INGREDIENTS
225 g/8 oz pork fillet
15 ml/1 tbsp light soy sauce
5 ml/1 tsp light brown sugar
5 ml/1 tsp Chinese rice wine or dry sherry
10 ml/2 tsp cornflour paste
115 g/4 oz mangetouts
115 g/4 oz/2 cups white mushrooms
1 medium or 2 small carrots
1 spring onion
60 ml/4 tbsp vegetable oil
5 ml/1 tsp salt
Basic Stock or water, if necessary
few drops of sesame oil

1 Cut the pork into thin slices about 4 x 2.5 cm/1½ x 1 in. Marinate the slices with about 5 ml/1 tsp of the soy sauce, the sugar, wine or sherry and cornflour paste.

2 Top and tail the mangetouts and thinly slice the mushrooms. Cut the carrots into pieces that are roughly the same size as the pork slices, and cut the spring onion into short sections.

3 Heat the oil in a preheated wok or frying pan and stir-fry the pieces of pork for about 1 minute, or until the colour changes. Remove the pork with a slotted spoon and keep warm.

4 Stir-fry the mangetouts, mushrooms and carrots for about 2 minutes, add the salt and the pork, and a little stock or water only if necessary. Continue stirring for another minute or so, then add the remaining soy sauce and blend well. Sprinkle with the sesame oil and serve.

Dry fried Shredded Beef

Dry frying is a Sichuan cooking method – the main ingredient is stir-fried over a low heat until dry, then finished off over a high heat.

Serves 4

INGREDIENTS
350–400 g/12–14 oz fillet or rump steak
1 large or 2 small carrots
2–3 stalks celery
30 ml/2 tbsp sesame oil
15 ml/1 tbsp Chinese rice wine or dry sherry
15 ml/1 tbsp chilli bean paste
15 ml/1 tbsp light soy sauce
1 garlic clove, finely chopped
5 ml/1 tsp light brown sugar
2–3 spring onions, finely chopped
2.5 ml/½ tsp finely chopped fresh root ginger
ground Sichuan peppercorns, to taste

3 Pour off the excess liquid and reserve. Continue stirring until the meat is absolutely dry.

1 With a Chinese cleaver or sharp knife, cut the beef into matchstick-size strips. Shred the carrots and celery.

2 Heat the sesame oil in a preheated wok (it will smoke very quickly). Reduce the heat and stir-fry the beef shreds with the rice wine or sherry until the colour changes.

4 Add the chilli bean paste, soy sauce, garlic and sugar to the wok, stir to blend well, then add the carrot and celery shreds.

5 Increase the heat to high and add the spring onions, ginger and the reserved liquid. Continue stirring, and when all the juice has evaporated, season with Sichuan pepper and serve.

Stir-fried Beef & Broccoli

This spicy beef dish is both attractive and easy to prepare. It may be
served either with noodles or on a bed of freshly boiled rice.

Serves 4

INGREDIENTS
350 g/12 oz rump or lean prime
    casserole steak
15 ml/1 tbsp cornflour
5 ml/1 tsp sesame oil
350 g/12 oz broccoli, cut into small florets
4 spring onions, diagonally sliced
1 carrot, cut into matchstick strips
1 garlic clove, crushed
2.5 cm/1 in piece root ginger, cut into
    very fine strips
120 ml/4 fl oz/½ cup Basic Stock
30 ml/2 tbsp soy sauce
30 ml/2 tbsp dry sherry
10 ml/2 tsp soft light brown sugar
spring onion tassels, to garnish
noodles or rice, to serve

2 Heat the sesame oil in a large
frying pan or wok. Add the beef
strips and stir-fry over a brisk heat
for 3 minutes, until just cooked.
Remove the beef from the wok with
a slotted spoon and set aside but
keep warm.

3 Add the broccoli florets, sliced
spring onions, carrot strips, garlic,
ginger and stock to the wok. Cover
and leave to simmer for 3 minutes.
Remove the lid and continue to
cook, stirring constantly until all the
stock has reduced to about a couple
of tablespoons.

1 Using a sharp knife, trim the beef
and cut it into thin slices across
the grain. Cut each slice into thin
strips. Toss the strips in the cornflour
to coat thoroughly.

4 Mix the soy sauce, sherry and
brown sugar together in a bowl.
Add to the wok with the beef. Stir-fry
for 2–3 minutes, stirring constantly to
ensure even cooking.

5 Spoon into a warmed serving dish and garnish with the spring onion tassels. Serve immediately with boiled noodles or rice.

COOK'S TIP: To make spring onion tassels, trim the bulb base then cut the green shoot so that the onion is 7.5 cm/3 in long. Shred to within 2.5 cm/1 in of the base and put into iced water for 1 hour.

Beef with Peppers

A spicy, rich dish in which the distinctive flavour of black bean sauce plays a major part. This is always a popular recipe.

Serves 4

INGREDIENTS
350 g/12 oz rump steak, trimmed and
    thinly sliced
15 ml/1 tbsp vegetable oil
300 ml/½ pint/1¼ cups Basic Stock
2 garlic cloves, finely chopped
5 ml/1 tsp grated fresh root ginger
1 fresh red chilli, seeded and
    finely chopped
15 ml/1 tbsp black bean sauce
1 green pepper, cored, seeded and cut into
    2.5 cm/1 in squares
15 ml/1 tbsp Chinese rice wine or
    dry sherry
5 ml/1 tsp cornflour
5 ml/1 tsp caster sugar
45 ml/3 tbsp water
salt
rice noodles, to serve

2 Bring the stock to the boil in a saucepan. Add the beef and cook for 2 minutes, stirring constantly. Drain the beef and set aside.

3 Heat the remaining oil in a preheated wok. Stir-fry the garlic, ginger and chilli with the black bean sauce for a few seconds. Add the pepper and a little water. Cook for about 2 minutes more, then stir in the rice wine or sherry. Add the beef slices and spoon the sauce over.

4 Mix the cornflour and sugar to a paste with the water. Pour the mixture into the pan. Cook, stirring, until thickened. Season with salt. Serve at once, with rice noodles.

COOK'S TIP: For extra colour, use half each of a green pepper and red pepper or a mixture that includes yellow and orange.

1 Place the steak in a medium-size bowl. Add 5 ml/1 tsp of the vegetable oil and stir to coat.

Pak Choi with Oyster Sauce

Pak choi is prepared in a very simple way – stir-fried and served with oyster sauce. The combination makes a simple and tasty accompaniment.

Serves 3–4

INGREDIENTS
450 g/1 lb pak choi
30 ml/2 tbsp groundnut oil
15–30 ml/1–2 tbsp oyster sauce

2 Heat the groundnut oil in a preheated wok or large frying pan. Add the pak choi pieces and stir-fry for 2–3 minutes, until the leaves have started to wilt.

1 Trim the pak choi, removing any discoloured leaves and damaged stems. Tear into manageable pieces.

COOK'S TIP: Vegetarian oyster-flavoured sauce is available from Chinese supermarkets.

VARIATION: For a change you can replace the pak choi with choi sam, or Chinese flowering cabbage. It has bright green leaves and tiny yellow flowers. It is available from Chinese supermarkets.

3 Add the oyster sauce and continue to stir-fry for a few seconds more, until the pak choi is cooked but still slightly crisp to the bite. Transfer to a serving dish and serve immediately.

Broccoli with Soy Sauce

The broccoli cooks in next to no time, so don't start cooking until you are almost ready to eat.

Serves 4

INGREDIENTS
450 g/1 lb broccoli
15 ml/1 tbsp vegetable oil
2 garlic cloves, crushed
2 garlic cloves, sliced
30 ml/2 tbsp light soy sauce
salt

1 Using a sharp knife, trim the thick stems of the broccoli and discard. Cut the broccoli head into florets, which should be fairly large, leaving a short stalk. Rinse and dry thoroughly.

2 Bring a large saucepan of lightly salted water to the boil. Add the broccoli florets and cook them for 3–4 minutes until they have become slightly tender but still retain a definite crispness.

3 Drain the broccoli thoroughly in a colander and arrange in a warm serving dish. Keep warm while you prepare the garlic.

4 Heat the oil in a small saucepan. Fry the crushed garlic for 2 minutes to release the flavour, then remove it with a slotted spoon. Fry the slices of garlic in the oil and set aside for the garnish.

5 Pour the oil carefully over the broccoli, taking care as it will splatter. Drizzle the soy sauce over the broccoli, scatter over the slices of fried garlic and serve.

VARIATION: Most leafy vegetables taste delicious prepared this way. Try blanched cos lettuce for a change.

Black Bean & Vegetable Stir-fry

The secret of a quick stir-fry is to prepare all the ingredients first.
This colourful vegetable mixture is coated in a classic Chinese sauce.

Serves 4

INGREDIENTS
8 spring onions
225 g/8 oz/2 cups button mushrooms
1 red pepper
1 green pepper
2 large carrots
60 ml/4 tbsp sesame oil
2 garlic cloves, crushed
60 ml/4 tbsp black bean sauce
90 ml/6 tbsp warm water
225 g/8 oz/1 cup beansprouts
salt and freshly ground black pepper

1 Thinly slice the spring onions into narrow matchsticks and thinly slice the button mushrooms.

2 Cut both the peppers in half, remove the seeds and slice the flesh into thin strips.

3 Cut the carrots in half. Cut each half into thin strips lengthways. Stack the slices and cut through them to make very fine strips.

4 Heat the oil in a large preheated wok or frying pan until very hot. Add the spring onions and garlic, and stir-fry for 30 seconds.

5 Add the mushrooms, peppers and carrots. Stir-fry over a high heat for 5–6 minutes, until the vegetables are just beginning to soften.

6 Mix the black bean sauce with the water. Add to the wok or pan and cook for 3–4 minutes. Stir in the beansprouts and stir-fry for 1 minute more, until all the vegetables are coated in the sauce. Season to taste. Serve at once.

Tofu & Crunchy Vegetables

High-protein tofu is nicest if marinated before cooking. Smoked tofu is even tastier.

Serves 4

INGREDIENTS
2 x 225 g/8 oz cartons smoked tofu (beancurd), cubed
45 ml/3 tbsp soy sauce
30 ml/2 tbsp Chinese rice wine or dry sherry
15 ml/1 tbsp sesame oil
45 ml/3 tbsp groundnut or sunflower oil
2 leeks, thinly sliced
2 carrots, cut in sticks
1 large courgette, thinly sliced
115 g/4 oz baby sweetcorn, halved
115 g/4 oz/1½ cups button or shiitake mushrooms, sliced
15 ml/1 tbsp sesame seeds
1 packet of egg noodles, cooked and tossed in sesame oil, to serve

1 Marinate the tofu in the soy sauce, rice wine or sherry and sesame oil for at least 10 minutes. Drain and reserve the marinade.

2 Heat the groundnut or sunflower oil in a preheated wok and stir-fry the tofu cubes until browned all over. Remove and reserve.

3 Stir-fry the leeks, carrots, courgette and baby corn, stirring and tossing for about 2 minutes. Add the mushrooms and cook for 1 minute more.

4 Return the tofu to the wok and pour in the marinade. Heat until bubbling, then scatter over the sesame seeds.

5 Serve as soon as possible with the hot cooked noodles, dressed in a little sesame oil.

Braised Chinese Vegetables

The original recipe calls for 18 different ingredients to represent the
18 Buddhas, but nowadays between four and six are quite sufficient.

Serves 4

INGREDIENTS
10 g/¼ oz dried wood-ears
75 g/3 oz straw mushrooms, drained
50 g/2 oz mangetouts
1 cake tofu (beancurd)
175 g/6 oz Chinese leaves
45–60 ml/3–4 tbsp vegetable oil
75 g/3 oz sliced bamboo shoots, drained
5 ml/1 tsp salt
2.5 ml/½ tsp light brown sugar
15 ml/1 tbsp light soy sauce
few drops sesame oil (optional)

1 Soak the wood-ears in cold water
for 15 minutes, then rinse and
discard the hard stalks, if any. Cut the
straw mushrooms in half lengthways,
if they are large – keep whole, if they
are small. Top and tail the mangetouts.
Cut the tofu into about 12 small
pieces. Cut the Chinese leaves into
small pieces the same size as the
trimmed mangetouts.

2 Harden the tofu pieces by placing
them in a pan of boiling water for
about 2 minutes. Remove and drain.

3 Heat the oil in a flameproof
casserole or saucepan and lightly
brown the tofu. Remove with a slotted
spoon and keep warm.

4 Stir-fry all the vegetables for about
1½ minutes, then add the tofu, salt,
sugar and soy sauce. Continue stirring
for another minute, then cover and
braise for 2–3 minutes. Sprinkle with
sesame oil (if using) and serve.

Spicy Sichuan Noodles

This is a filling noodle salad with an unusual spicy dressing.

Serves 4

INGREDIENTS
350 g/12 oz thick noodles
175 g/6 oz cooked chicken, shredded
50 g/2 oz/⅓ cup roasted cashew nuts

FOR THE DRESSING
4 spring onions, chopped
30 ml/2 tbsp chopped fresh coriander
2 garlic cloves, chopped
30 ml/2 tbsp smooth peanut butter
30 ml/2 tbsp sweet chilli sauce
15 ml/1 tbsp soy sauce
15 ml/1 tbsp rice vinegar
15 ml/1 tbsp sesame oil
30 ml/2 tbsp olive oil
30 ml/2 tbsp chicken or vegetable stock
10 toasted Sichuan peppercorns, ground

1 Cook the noodles until just tender, following the packet directions. Drain, rinse under cold, running water and drain well.

2 While the noodles are cooking, combine all the dressing ingredients in a bowl and whisk well. Add the noodles, shredded chicken and cashew nuts, toss gently and adjust the seasoning. Serve at once.

Sesame Noodles with Spring Onions

Prepare this simple but very tasty warm salad in minutes.

Serves 4

INGREDIENTS
2 garlic cloves, roughly chopped
30 ml/2 tbsp Chinese sesame paste
15 ml/1 tbsp dark sesame oil
30 ml/2 tbsp soy sauce
30 ml/2 tbsp Chinese rice wine or dry sherry
15 ml/1 tbsp clear honey
pinch of five-spice powder
350 g/12 oz soba or buckwheat noodles
4 spring onions, finely sliced diagonally
50 g/2 oz/¼ cup beansprouts
7.5 cm/3 in piece of cucumber, cut into matchsticks
toasted sesame seeds
salt and freshly ground black pepper

1 Process the garlic, sesame paste, oil, soy sauce, rice wine or sherry, honey and five-spice powder with seasoning in a blender or food processor.

2 Cook the noodles until just tender. Drain and tip into a bowl. Toss with the dressing and the spring onions. Top with the beansprouts, cucumber and sesame seeds, and serve.

Right: Spicy Sichuan Noodles (top); Sesame Noodles with Spring Onions

Plain Rice

Use long grain or patna rice, or fragrant Thai rice. Allow 50 g/ 2 oz/⅓ cup raw rice per person.

Serves 4

INGREDIENTS
225 g/8 oz/1⅓ cups rice
about 250 ml/8 fl oz/1 cup cold water
2.5 ml/½ tsp vegetable oil
salt

1 Wash and rinse the rice. Place the rice in a saucepan and add the water. There should be no more than 2 cm/¾ in water above the surface of the rice.

2 Bring to the boil, add the oil and a pinch of salt, then stir to prevent the rice sticking to the base of the pan. Reduce the heat to very low, cover and cook for 15–20 minutes.

3 Remove the pan from the heat and leave it to stand for 10 minutes. Fluff up the rice with a fork or spoon just before serving.

Egg Fried Rice

This is a favourite accompaniment to many Chinese dishes. It is best to use rice with a fairly firm texture.

Serves 4

INGREDIENTS
3 eggs
5 ml/1 tsp salt
2 spring onions, finely chopped
30–45 ml/2–3 tbsp vegetable oil
450 g/1 lb/2⅔ cups cooked rice
115 g/4 oz/1 cup green peas

1 In a bowl, lightly beat the eggs with a pinch of the salt and a few pieces of the spring onions.

2 Heat the oil in a preheated wok, add the eggs and cook until lightly scrambled.

3 Add the rice and stir to make sure that the grains are separated. Add the remaining salt, spring onions and peas. Blend well and serve.

Right: Plain Rice (top); Egg Fried Rice

Index

Beef: Beef with Peppers, 48–9
Dry fried Shredded Beef, 44–5
Stir-fried Broccoli &, 46–7
Black Bean & Vegetable Stir-fry, 54–5
Broccoli with Soy Sauce, 52–3

Chicken: Chicken with Chinese Vegetables, 34–5
"Kung Po" Chicken – Sichuan Style, 32–3
Shredded Chicken with Celery, 34–5
Chow Mein, Pork, 41
Corn & Crabmeat Soup, 10–11
Crab: Corn & Crabmeat Soup, 10–11
Crab Spring Rolls, 18–19

Duck, Stir-fried Crispy, 36–7

Eggs: Egg Flower Soup, 13

Egg Fried Rice, 62–3

Fish: Braised Whole Fish in Chilli & Garlic Sauce, 24–5
Fish with Sweet & Sour Sauce, 22–3
Red Snapper with Ginger & Spring Onions, 20–1
Three Sea Flavours Stir-fry, 26–7
Flavourings, 6–7

Hot & Sour Soup, 12

"Kung Po" Chicken – Sichuan Style, 32–3

Noodles: Sesame Noodles with Spring Onions, 60–1
Spicy Sichuan Noodles, 60–1

Pak Choi with Oyster Sauce, 50–1
Pork: Ginger Pork with Black Bean Sauce, 40
Pork Chow Mein, 41

Stir-fried Pork with Vegetables, 42–3
Sweet & Sour Pork, 38–9
Prawns, Stir-fried with Mangetouts, 28–9

Red Snapper with Ginger & Spring Onions, 20–1
Rice: Egg Fried Rice, 62–3
Plain Rice, 62–3

Seafood Wontons with Coriander Dressing, 14–15
"Seaweed", Crispy, 16–17
Soups, 10–13
Spices, 6–7
Spring Greens: Crispy "Seaweed", 16–17
Spring Rolls, Crab, 18–19
Squid: Stir-fried Five-spice Squid with Black Bean Sauce, 30–1
Stir-frying, 8
Stock, 9

Three Sea Flavours

Stir-fry, 26–7
Tofu & Crunchy Vegetables, 56–7

Vegetables: Black Bean & Vegetable Stir-fry, 54–5
Braised Chinese Vegetables, 58–9
Tofu & Crunchy Vegetables, 56–7

Woks, seasoning, 9
Wontons, Seafood, 14–15

This edition is published by Hermes House

© Anness Publishing Limited 1999, updated 2001, 2002.

Hermes House is an imprint of Anness Publishing Limited,
Hermes House, 88–89 Blackfriars Road, London SE1 8HA

All rights reserved. No part of this publication may be reproduced, stored in a retrieval system,
or transmitted in any way or by any means, electronic, mechanical, photocopying, recording or otherwise,
without the prior written permission of the copyright holder.

Publisher: Joanna Lorenz
Editor: Valerie Ferguson
Series Designer: Bobbie Colgate Stone
Designer: Andrew Heath
Production Controller: Joanna King

Recipes contributed by: Catherine Atkinson, Kit Chan,
Roz Denny, Matthew Drennan, Sarah Edmonds,
Shirley Gill, Deh-Ta Hsiung, Lesley Mackley,
Kathy Mann, Liz Trigg

Photography: William Adams-Lingwood, Karl Adamson,
Edward Allwright, James Duncan, Michelle Garrett,
Amanda Heywood, Michael Michaels,
Thomas Odulate

Notes:
For all recipes, quantities are given in both metric and imperial measures and, where appropriate, measures are also given in standard cups and spoons.
Follow one set, but not a mixture, because they are not interchangeable.

Standard spoon and cup measures are level.

1 tsp = 5 ml   1 tbsp =15 ml   1 cup = 250 ml/8 fl oz

Australian standard tablespoons are 20 ml.
Australian readers should use 3 tsp in place of 1 tbsp for measuring small quantities of gelatine, cornflour, salt, etc.

Medium eggs are used unless otherwise stated.

3 5 7 9 10 8 6 4

Printed in China